BILTMORE

by William A.V. Cecil

The Vision and Reality of George W. Vanderbilt,
Richard Morris Hunt and Frederick Law Olmsted.

Biltmore Estate—Asheville, North Carolina

Biltmore House, located in the western mountains of North Carolina, just outside of Asheville, has been called many things by many people. One of the more common names has been *"a white elephant"* but others call it *"America's finest home"* . . . *"Olmsted's masterpiece"* . . . *"Vanderbilt's folly"* . . . *"Hunt's dream castle."*

RGE W. VANDERBILT

What is Biltmore Estate? The answer is very simple—it is one of the finest *"National Historic Sites"* in the United States today. Not only that, it is becoming of greater interest to our fellow citizens as well as to our historians, architects and other scholars as the years go by. Why do we

RICHARD MORRIS HUNT

say this? Simply because today Biltmore House, surrounded by the original 10,000 acres of the Estate, has not only been completely maintained, but has just emerged from adolescence into maturity.

As far as large houses go in the United States, Biltmore has a certain

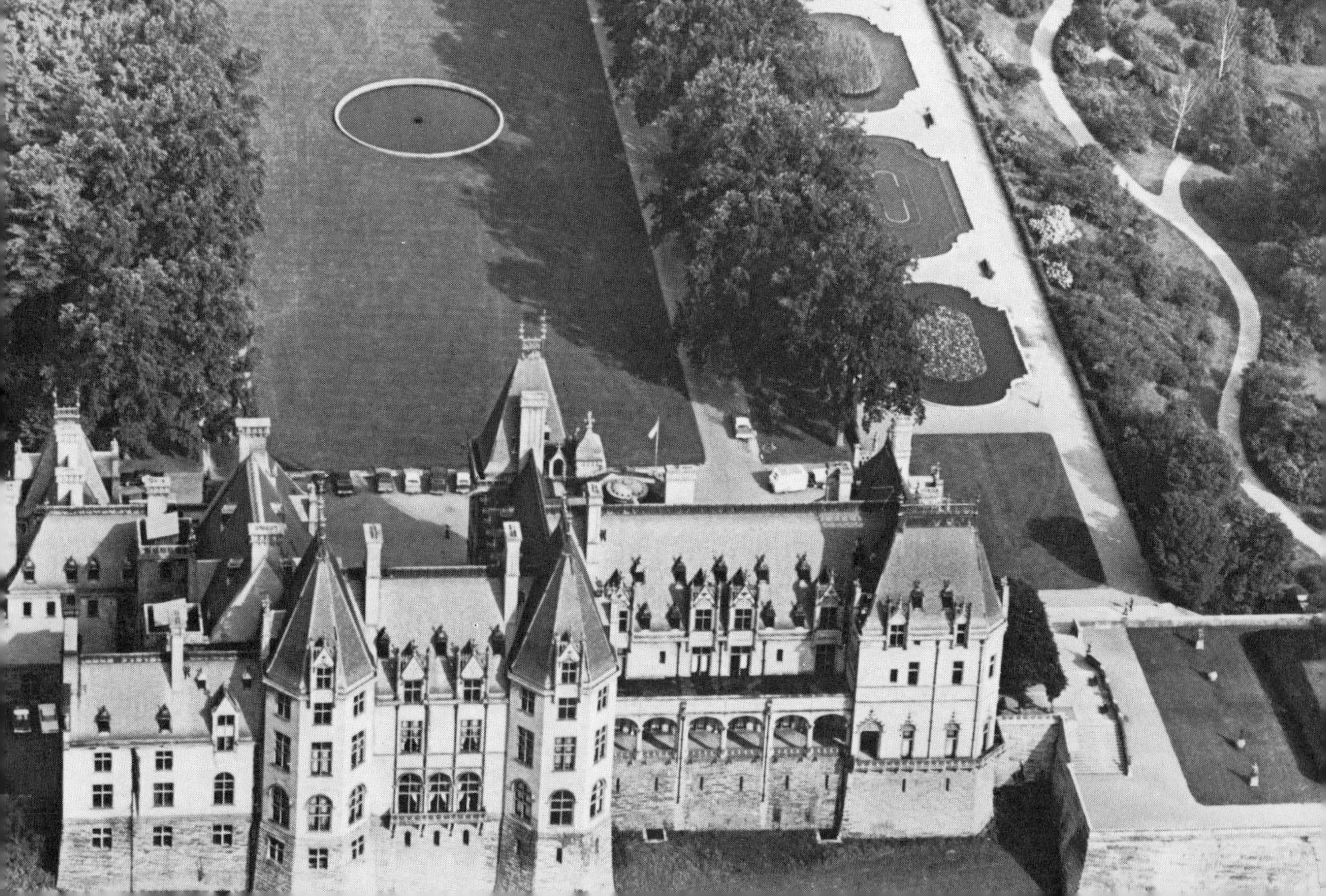

CHAUNCEY DELOS BEADLE

FREDERICK LAW OLMSTED

amount of age—seventy-seven years as of 1972—but compared to her European counterparts she is but an infant. Even before construction started in 1890—at the height of America's building spree—George Vanderbilt's agents were acquiring land to make possible the construction of his *"summer*

GIFFORD PINCHOT

DR. CARL A. SCHENCK

home.'' By the time Richard Morris Hunt was engaged as architect and Frederick Law Olmsted as landscape architect, the original project was beginning to change. Mr. Vanderbilt at the tender age of twenty-two, was, with the help of his above named friends, going to build a southern home,

probably red brick, white columns
and large porches. Be that as it may,
it soon became evident that other
forces were at work which would change
all these plans.

To start, George Vanderbilt
travelled abroad extensively and
during these travels he acquired objects

of art which would in no way actually fit into a small southern home. Secondly, Mr. Hunt was pleasantly encouraging these acquisitions as friends—close friends will do. Thirdly, Mr. Olmsted's commissions in the United States were of a size which would dwarf any residence not built to scale.

As all these factors came together
one lynch-pin finalized the development.
The site chosen for the land holdings
easily swayed any thoughts left about
the wisdom of building a *"French Chateau"*
in America. How easy it was to visualize
the Loire lazily coursing her way
through the bottom lands of Western North

Carolina. What a magnificent location, the finished castle overlooking the French Broad River, and beyond rolling pastures, parks and hills. In the far distance the Blue Ridge Mountains rising majestically yet peacefully. These factors then sealed the design fate of Biltmore.

By 1890 the lands were acquired and soon thereafter the project started. Not only was Biltmore House to be built, but the Estate was to be landscaped and a village constructed. First things first. While excavation and land preparation was going on, a railroad spur was built to the site from

Asheville. This line was purely to carry workers and materials to and from the construction area. It was obliterated upon completion of the project.

The village of Biltmore was built, houses for the staff, an office still used today, All Soul's Church for

worship, a railroad station, shops for
retail purchases, brick factories,
saw mills and so forth.

Nursery stock was planted in
preparation for inclusion in Olmsted's
final masterpiece. The project was
underway. Over a thousand artisans and
workers partook in the labours of

Biltmore. Indeed the first major
employer in the area was George Vanderbilt.
Even today amongst the honored families
in the western counties of Buncombe,
Henderson and Haywood, many is the
descendant whose parents or
grandparents first received employment
on Biltmore Estate.

While all this was proceeding, more plans were being made. Biltmore was not just a *"rich man's folly,"* or a social *"one upmanship,"* it was to be a working estate, modeled on the European concept. Thus came into being truck farms for fresh produce, Jersey cattle and planned forests.

By 1895 Biltmore House was complete. Frederick Law Olmsted's plantings were pretty much in place, the truck farm provided fresh produce, the Jersey herd fresh milk, the greenhouses fresh fruits and the land was productive.

Although wealth was taken for granted by the collaborating colleagues

and taxation was still a factor of
the future, it was beginning to be
apparent that the scale of development
was so great as to cause some anxiety.
In Olmsted's area, he had planned
an Arboretum Road to encircle the
property. This was all laid out but
never planted to completion. One

room in Biltmore House was never finished and seeds of dissent appeared in the early 1910's in the forestry areas. Gifford Pinchot and Carl Schenck joined the vast talent which Mr. Vanderbilt assembled, and dissembled. Each left his mark on the future. Each laid the groundwork for the maturity of Biltmore.

The continuity of management was assured in the employment by Olmsted, of Chauncey Delos Beadle, his assistant. Mr. Beadle, so the story goes, was hired for two years as planting superintendent but died in 1950 at the age of 83, never having left Biltmore.

Changes did occur. As they did in the world, so they did at Biltmore.

Mr. Vanderbilt died in 1914 in Washington, D.C., following an appendectomy. World War I reared its ugly head, income and inheritance taxes took their place in American's lives and fortunes.

Mrs. Vanderbilt, now a widow, deeded some 120 thousand acres of forest

land holdings to the United States, and Pisgah National Forest had a nucleus upon which to grow. Judge Junius G. Adams, a brilliant attorney in Asheville, was engaged by Mrs. Vanderbilt as overall counsellor.

In 1932 Adams changed Biltmore from a personal property into a private

corporation and Biltmore House opened
her doors to the public. The stage
was set for adolescence. By now the
plantings of Olmsted were growing
and completed to the revised plans.
The Jersey herd was amongst the finest
in the United States and Biltmore
Dairy Farms under E.D. Mitchell was
becoming an outstanding regional dairy.

The forestry school and the Biltmore plantings were mainly in the Pisgah National Forest under National Forest supervision and control, but research and sustained yield harvests were still conducted on Biltmore Estate.

World War II created havoc. If the depression had set the stage for

difficult growth, World War II all but killed the opportunity for continued prosperity—certainly as far as tourism was concerned. Gasoline rationing forced the closing of Biltmore House as a tourist attraction.

From adversity comes opportunity. In exchange for visitors, Biltmore

House played host to the Art Treasures
of the United States. Down from
Washington's National Gallery of Art
came America's masterpieces for
safekeeping. Down from Boston came ladies
to repair the magnificent tapestries.
Up to Washington, New York and overseas,
both East and West, went some of the
finest of America's young men to fight
the common enemy.

The post holocaust era began. Out of Detroit came vehicles not for war—but for peace. Biltmore House reopened her doors. Roads which Olmsted in 1893 had planned to have *"macadamized"* were now paved. Mr. Beadle still collected azaleas, Judge Adams and E.D. Mitchell still saw that the

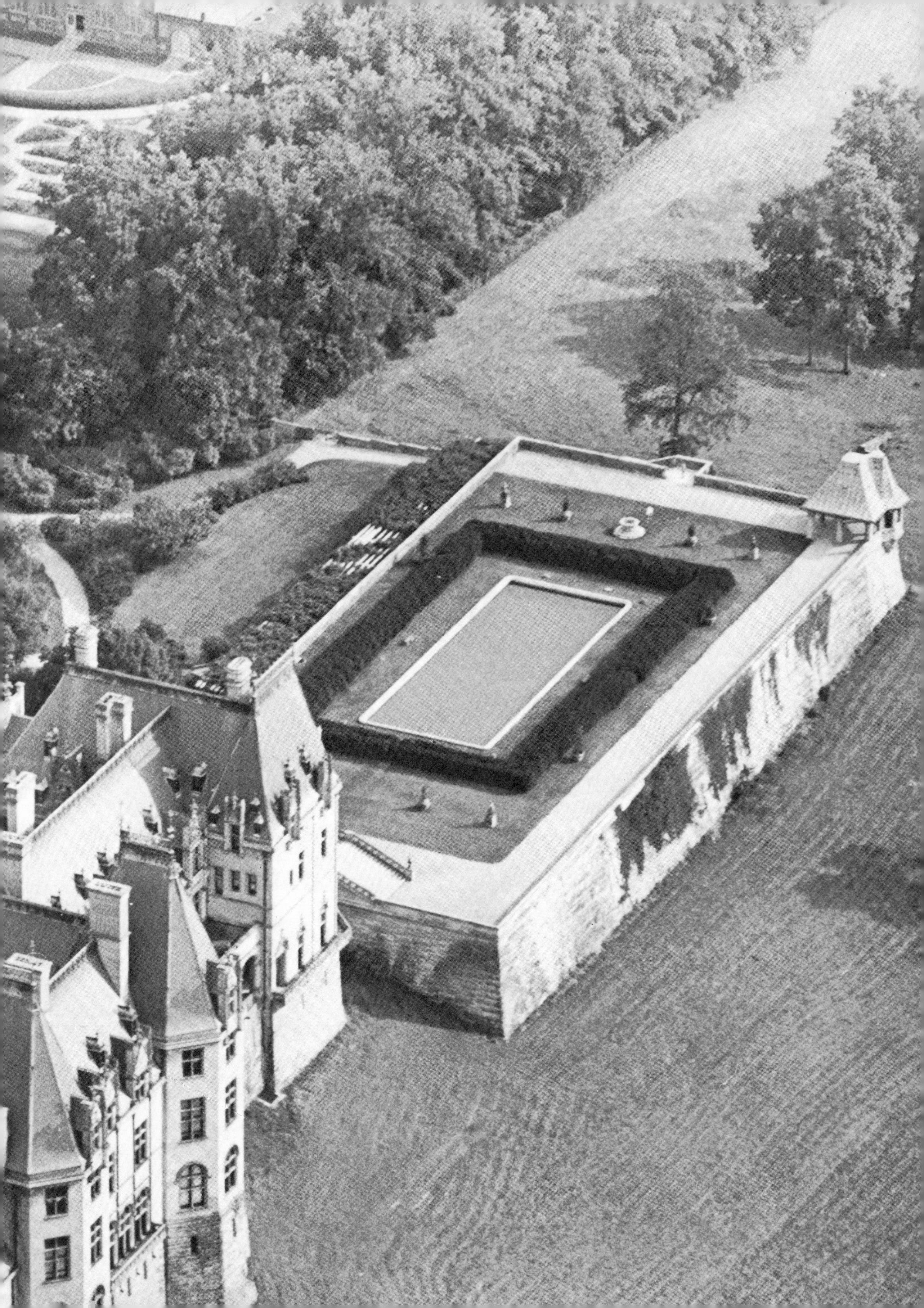

Dairy, the farming and the forestry operations prospered and Biltmore House cast her early morning shadows on the banks of the French Broad River.

It was not a return to serenity. It was a challenge in a changing world. Management of Biltmore became all important. Of utmost importance was

the realization that here was an estate
of national and eventually international
importance. Tremendous talent in the
late 19th century had been garnered
to produce an outstanding Estate, with
the potential of realizing George
Vanderbilt's dream of self-sufficiency,
in a world vastly different from

the one in which he and his colleagues had lived, built, planned and dreamed.

Today, Hunt's Biltmore House still stands—her shadows proud, her requirements demanding, but in these requirements lie her salvation and her survival.

Gone are the days of *"dollar-a-day"* wages, upon us are the years of taxes and national outmigration from rural

areas to urban cities. The difficulties of marrying the old with the new—the stark interstates with the gentle curves of Olmsted's roadways—these are the problems of progress which must be solved—not stemmed.

As in Olmsted's lifetime so in the latter half of the twentieth century, planning for the future, not just for the present, is the rule.

As Olmsted laid out the grounds, his vision and guiding hand can still be seen and felt.

The fantastic logic of these original thoughts—to say nothing of the mature beauty of the present day Estate—really is the true inheritance which a group of remarkable men gave to the inheritors.

If vision is given to any of us and
if any of us have the wisdom to use it,
the *"lady on the hill"* shows that
survival in our day and age is not only
possible but certain. Not in any
retrogressive sense, but with confidence
that all need not be temporary and
mundane; that preservation of the good of
our ancestors for the benefit of our
descendants is truly the American reality.

EDITOR: William A.V. Cecil DESIGN: William M. Guillet

PHOTOGRAPHY: *The Biltmore Company;* Carl D. Burleson, W. A. V. Cecil. *Asheville Citizen-Times Publishing Company;* Malcolm Gamble, page 3, June Glenn, Jr., pages 11, 74, 75 (top), Bert Shipman, pages 16 (top right), 68, 75 (bottom), 79. *U.S. Forest Service;* page 12.

LITHOGRAPHY: Kingsport Press, Inc., Kingsport, Tennessee